Struik Pocket Guides
for Southern Africa

Common Birds

Ian Sinclair
(Author of *Field Guide to the
Birds of Southern Africa*)

ILLUSTRATED BY
Penny Meakin
and Douglas Goode

STRUIK

D0068220

Contents

Struik Publishers (Pty) Ltd
(a member of The Struik New Holland Publishing Group (Pty) Ltd)
Cornelis Struik House
80 McKenzie Street
Cape Town 8001

Reg. No.: 54/00965/07

First published 1990, reprinted in 1993
Second edition 1994

10 9 8 7 6 5 4

Copyright © text: J.C. Sinclair 1990, 1994
Copyright © illustrations: P. Meakin and D. Goode 1990, 1994

DTP setting by Jenny Camons
Reproduction by Fotoplate (Pty) Ltd, Cape Town
Printing and binding by CTP Book Printers (Pty) Ltd

ISBN 1 86825 505 0

Introduction

Of the approximately 900 species of birds that occur in southern Africa, 130 are represented in this guide. The birds chosen are not necessarily the most common in the region, but rather those which are conspicuous or common either in the major centres or in the bigger game reserves. Virtually any outdoor excursion, be it a visit to the local playground, a day-trip to the seaside, or an annual holiday to a game reserve, provides the opportunity to see a variety of birds. Birdwatching in these environments can be done very casually and with minimum effort, and by having this guide at hand, you will be able to identify many of the birds around you.

Do not feel hindered if you live in one of the major towns or cities of the region: in any one day, depending on the season, you should be able to identify more than 20 different bird species with ease. Should you live in a smaller town in the countryside, your chances of seeing a wider range of birds are greatly increased, while living near thick bushveld will afford the opportunity to view different bird species in abundance. The seaside, with its rocky headlands, estuaries and beaches, offers its own particular range of birds, many of which would not be seen in freshwater areas inland. However, for those without access to the coast, a visit to a local marsh or dam will itself provide an astonishing variety of birds.

The diversity and number of birds in an area is dependent on the type of vegetation and the various habitats associated with it; obviously, the less disturbed by humans an area is, the greater the variety and quantity of birdlife there will be. The map below shows the major vegetation zones of southern Africa. For a fuller discussion of vegetation and habitat, and the birds associated with different areas, see page 49 'Birdwatching by habitat'.

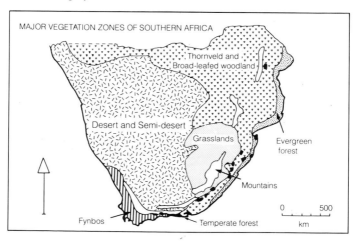

MAJOR VEGETATION ZONES OF SOUTHERN AFRICA

Thornveld and Broad-leafed woodland

Desert and Semi-desert

Grasslands

Evergreen forest

Mountains

Fynbos

Temperate forest

0   500
km

3

How to use this book

This guide is specifically designed to help you identify a selection of birds as quickly, accurately and confidently as possible. The colour illustrations are the main guide to identification and depict the birds in the plumages in which you are most likely to see them. Where there are significant differences between the sexes and adult or immature, then both or all individuals have been illustrated where space has allowed. The brief accounts that accompany the illustrations highlight the most important field characters and, if relevant, make reference to the habitat, call and distribution of the bird. Each account is followed by a length measurement. This does not indicate the height of the bird, but is taken from the tip of the bill to the tip of the tail of an out-stretched bird, but where a bird has an exceptionally long bill or tail, these features have not been included in the overall measurement. The reason for this becomes clear when one considers a Pintailed Whydah (about the size of a Redbilled Quelea) against a Feral Pigeon: the length of the whydah including its long tail is equal to that of the much larger pigeon, while the length measurement excluding the tail gives a far more realistic idea of the whydah's real size.

Familiarize yourself with the illustrations and take note of the distribution and preferred habitat of different species. If you cannot identify a particular bird in the field, try to establish to which family it belongs: is it a starling, a sparrow, a gull or a sugarbird, for example. If you are able to determine this, you can turn to the relevant section of the book and through a simple process of elimination should be able to identify the bird. Often time is of essence in the field, however, and you may not have time to check through the book. Therefore, it is a good idea to take along a pencil and sketch-pad, and to jot down notes and make a simple sketch of the bird, observing the most obvious field characters: length of the bill, tail and legs, striking colour patterns or markings and where they occur, and general size and shape. Size can be very tricky to determine in the field, especially if you are viewing the bird through binoculars. Establish this by mentally comparing the bird's size to that of a bird with which you are familiar (a chicken, sparrow or pigeon).

An important aspect of bird identification is habitat. By knowing the type of habitat in which you are birdwatching and the birds most likely to occur there, your chances of correct identification will be greatly enhanced. For example, it would be foolish to look for a Blackbrowed Albatross at the Vaal Dam, but quite realistic to expect to see a Reed Cormorant there. Make use of the distribution maps alongside each species, as these will advise you immediately as to whether a particular bird occurs in your area or not.

Legends and abbreviations

ad. = adult	br. = breeding	$\female$ = female
imm. = immature	non-br. = non-breeding	$\male$ = male

Jackass Penguin

Confined mainly to off-shore islands in the Cape, but rarely seen at sea because it swims very low in the water showing only the black and white head pattern. Imm. lacks distinctive head pattern and is dark grey above. Endemic. 60 cm

black and white head diagnostic

Dabchick

Br. ad. distinguished by rufous head and neck, and by creamy-white spot at base of bill. Non-br. ad. and imm. are greyish-brown. In flight shows a broad white stripe on upper wing. 20 cm

distinctive pale spot

broad black border to underwing

Blackbrowed Albatross

A large sea-bird with long, narrow wings. Commonly seen in the vicinity of fishing boats and often comes close inshore during storms. Imm. has dusky collar and dark underwings. 90 cm

yellow bill

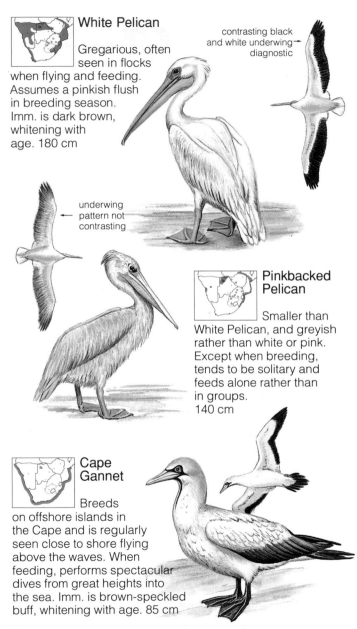

White Pelican

Gregarious, often seen in flocks when flying and feeding. Assumes a pinkish flush in breeding season. Imm. is dark brown, whitening with age. 180 cm

contrasting black and white underwing → diagnostic

← underwing pattern not contrasting

Pinkbacked Pelican

Smaller than White Pelican, and greyish rather than white or pink. Except when breeding, tends to be solitary and feeds alone rather than in groups. 140 cm

Cape Gannet

Breeds on offshore islands in the Cape and is regularly seen close to shore flying above the waves. When feeding, performs spectacular dives from great heights into the sea. Imm. is brown-speckled buff, whitening with age. 85 cm

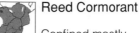

Reed Cormorant

Confined mostly to freshwater areas. Often seen perching with wings held outstretched. Imm., although also white below, is very much smaller than similar Whitebreasted Cormorant. 52 cm

long tail

orange patch brighter when breeding

Cape Cormorant

Most common of the cormorants and confined to coastal regions, especially of the Cape. May be seen in large groups, flying in line formations out at sea. Larger than Crowned Cormorant but smaller than Bank and Whitebreasted cormorants. Endemic. 65 cm

pronounced erectile crest

Crowned Cormorant

The marine equivalent of Reed Cormorant, occurring only on the west coast. Tail shorter than Reed Cormorant's and forehead has more pronounced crest. Imm. has brown underparts, not white as in Reed Cormorant. Endemic. 50 cm

Whitebreasted Cormorant

Much larger than other cormorants and with distinctive white breast and flank patches. Occurs in both marine and freshwater areas. Imm. has completely white underparts but is twice the size of similar imm. Reed Cormorant. 90 cm

long, egret-like neck →

Darter

Resembles a cormorant but has a much longer neck, a very long tail and a thin, pointed bill. Swims with body submerged and only snake-like neck and head held aloft. Imm. has pale underparts. 80 cm

naked pink sac

Marabou Stork

A large, ungainly bird with a very wide wingspan and a characteristic pink throat sac. Might be mistaken for a vulture in flight but long bill, and legs projecting beyond tail distinguish it. 150 cm

8

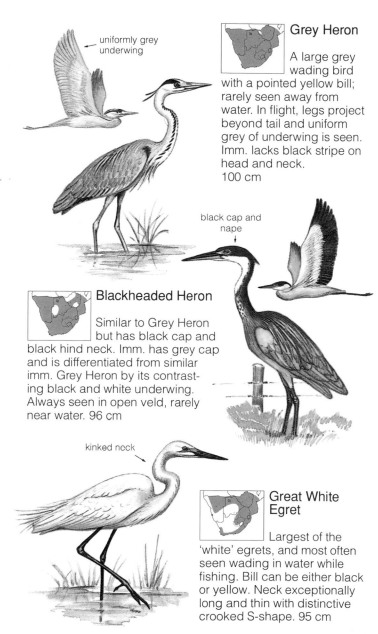

uniformly grey underwing

Grey Heron

A large grey wading bird with a pointed yellow bill; rarely seen away from water. In flight, legs project beyond tail and uniform grey of underwing is seen. Imm. lacks black stripe on head and neck.
100 cm

black cap and nape

Blackheaded Heron

Similar to Grey Heron but has black cap and black hind neck. Imm. has grey cap and is differentiated from similar imm. Grey Heron by its contrasting black and white underwing. Always seen in open veld, rarely near water. 96 cm

kinked neck

Great White Egret

Largest of the 'white' egrets, and most often seen wading in water while fishing. Bill can be either black or yellow. Neck exceptionally long and thin with distinctive crooked S-shape. 95 cm

Cattle Egret

Any egret seen in company with cattle or game will be this species. Birds typically fly in flocks, often in V-formation. Br. ad. has reddish legs and buff plumes on head, back and breast; non-br. ad. has greenish legs and all-white plumage. 54 cm

bright yellow toes

Little Egret

Occurs in both coastal and freshwater areas. Very busy when feeding, dashing to and fro in frantic manner, sometimes with wings outstretched. Black legs with bright yellow feet are diagnostic. 65 cm

hammer-shaped profile →

Hamerkop

A brown, medium-sized wading bird with a peculiar crest giving the head a distinctive hammer-shaped profile. In flight resembles bird of prey, but is distinguished by long legs which extend beyond tail. Builds a huge, haystack-like nest in trees. 56 cm

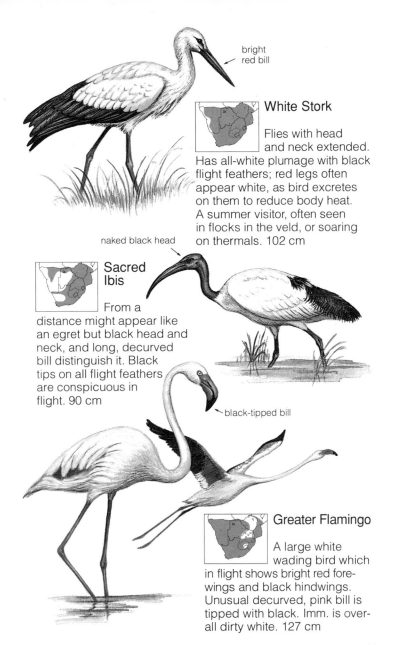

bright
red bill

White Stork

Flies with head and neck extended. Has all-white plumage with black flight feathers; red legs often appear white, as bird excretes on them to reduce body heat. A summer visitor, often seen in flocks in the veld, or soaring on thermals. 102 cm

naked black head

Sacred Ibis

From a distance might appear like an egret but black head and neck, and long, decurved bill distinguish it. Black tips on all flight feathers are conspicuous in flight. 90 cm

black-tipped bill

Greater Flamingo

A large white wading bird which in flight shows bright red fore-wings and black hindwings. Unusual decurved, pink bill is tipped with black. Imm. is over-all dirty white. 127 cm

Hadeda

A medium-sized, dark brown bird with a long, decurved bill. Bronze, iridescent shoulder patches are evident in bright sunlight . Loud 'ha ha ha dah da' call is distinctive. 76 cm

 — large grey head

Blue Crane

South Africa's national bird, common in various parts of the country. Greyish-blue with a long thin neck, an unusually large head, and elongated inner secondaries which give the impression of it having a long tail. Endemic. 100 cm

African Spoonbill

Very egret-like in shape and profile but long bill with flat, spoon-shaped end is distinctive. In flight keeps head and neck outstretched. When feeding sweeps bill from side to side through water. 90 cm

distinctive yellow bill

Yellowbilled Duck

A drab brown, mottled duck with a conspicuous yellow bill. Rectangular patch on wing – iridescent bluish-green and bordered with white – is visible in flight. 54 cm

Whitefaced Duck

The unusual upright stance, and black head and neck offset by a white face identify this bird. Three-note whistling call is distinctive. 48 cm

typical upright stance

Redbilled Teal

The pinkish-red bill and dark brown cap are diagnostic. Seen mostly in pairs or small groups on open water and small dams. Square, buff-coloured patches on wing are visible in flight. 48 cm

bald white patch

Redknobbed Coot

Very duck-like from a distance, with a small head and a white beak and forehead. Red knobs on forehead only apparent in breeding season when viewed at close range. 44 cm

13

Egyptian Goose

A brown goose, larger than most ducks and recognized by the dark brown patches around the eyes and the chestnut patch on the breast. In flight shows conspicuous white forewing patches and greenish hindwings. Occurs in most wetland areas. 70 cm

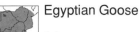

black and white head

red bill

Spurwinged Goose

A very large black goose with variable amounts of white on the head, neck and belly. In flight wings make loud 'whooshing' sound and bird utters a weak hissing and whistling note. Found on open water and in thick reedbeds. 100 cm

Southern Pochard

This small, dark brown duck appears black at long range. In flight shows a pale belly and a narrow white wing stripe. Female is paler than male and has white face markings. Bird habitually dives for food. 50 cm

♀

♂

African Fish Eagle

Occurs along large rivers and in coastal estuaries, and is often recognized by its characteristic yelping call. The white head and tail are diagnostic in ad.; imm. differs from ad., being mottled-brown with small white patches on the head and tail. 63-73 cm

Blackshouldered Kite

A small grey and white bird of prey with distinctive black shoulder patches. Commonly perches on telephone poles, sometimes flicking its white tail. When hunting, often hovers before spiralling down on to its prey. 33 cm

Tawny Eagle

A very large, dark brown eagle with a tawny-coloured head and shoulders. Mostly seen in game reserves and in bushveld. Imm. can be very much paler and may appear almost bleached. 65-80 cm

Rock Kestrel

A small falcon often seen hovering into the wind when hunting. Mostly associated with rocky hillsides and cliffs. Male is reddish with a blue-grey head and tail; female and imm. are more rufous and do not have blue-grey on head. 33-39 cm

♀

hovers when hunting

♂

colour may vary from light- to blackish-brown

Steppe Buzzard

A summer visitor from Asia with variable coloration, ranging from pale brown to almost black. Typical bird (as illustrated) shows pale bar across breast. 45-50 cm

African Goshawk

The rounded wings, long tail and small head mark this bird as a hawk and not a falcon. Ad. characterized by blue-grey upperparts and barred underparts; imm. is drabber and spotted below. Regularly soars over its territory uttering a short, sharp 'kwit' call. 36-39 cm

imm.

♂

♀

Yellowbilled Kite

A large, dark brown bird of prey with long wings and a characteristic forked tail. Ad. with all-yellow bill and cere; imm. has a black bill. Often seen patrolling roadways where it swoops to pick up animals killed by passing vehicles. 56 cm

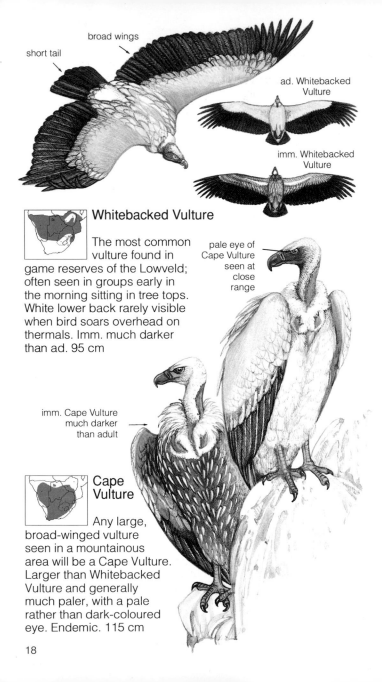

short tail

broad wings

ad. Whitebacked Vulture

imm. Whitebacked Vulture

Whitebacked Vulture

The most common vulture found in game reserves of the Lowveld; often seen in groups early in the morning sitting in tree tops. White lower back rarely visible when bird soars overhead on thermals. Imm. much darker than ad. 95 cm

pale eye of Cape Vulture seen at close range

imm. Cape Vulture much darker than adult

Cape Vulture

Any large, broad-winged vulture seen in a mountainous area will be a Cape Vulture. Larger than Whitebacked Vulture and generally much paler, with a pale rather than dark-coloured eye. Endemic. 115 cm

naked red skin on throat ⟶

Swainson's Francolin

A medium-sized francolin mostly found on agricultural lands and in open veld. Combined features of a red face and throat patch, and brown legs are diagnostic. Dark brown plumage is finely flecked with black. Endemic. 38 cm

dark cap can be held erect

Crested Francolin

A small, bantam-sized francolin with a dark cap and a broad white eyebrow stripe; frequently holds its tail cocked at 45° angle. Utters a characteristic crowing rattle from its thick bushveld habitat in the early morning. 33-35 cm

Black Korhaan

black head with white ear-patches distinctive

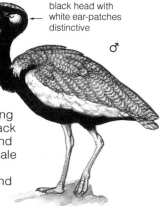

♂

Found and often heard in open veld, drawing attention through its loud, raucous call. Male is distinctive with a black head, neck and underparts, and contrasting white ear-patches. Female lacks black on head and neck and has a buff and brown back. In breeding season, male performs spectacular aerial display flight, slowly flapping wings to defend his territory. Endemic. 52 cm

speckled
black and
white

Cape Francolin

A large, rotund francolin, dark brown in colour, and common in fynbos of the western Cape; also occurs in pairs or small parties around edges of wheat fields. Pale grey cheeks give impression of it having a dark cap. Endemic. 42 cm

Natal Francolin

A dull, greyish-brown francolin with black and white speckled underparts, and distinctive reddish bill, legs and feet. Utters a loud and throaty crow at dawn and dusk. 35 cm

♂

Ostrich

An unmistakable, enormous, flightless bird. Male black and white; female brown and white, and imm. resembles female. Very young birds have black and white, spiky feathers on back. Height 2 m

Moorhen

sooty-grey plumage

Often seen swimming in open stretches of fresh water, showing jerky forward movements as it flicks its tail to reveal the white undertail. Smaller than a gallinule and with sooty-grey and brownish plumage and a yellow-tipped red bill. 32 cm

Purple Gallinule

large red bill

A chicken-sized bird found in reedbeds and swamps, with a large and conspicuous red bill, red legs and long toes. Ad. is purplish in colour with a turquoise neck and breast; imm. is dull brown. Typically creeps and clambers through reeds, or stalks over floating vegetation flicking its white undertail. 46 cm

Black Crake

bright yellow bill

A very small, all-black bird with bright red legs and toes, and an almost luminescent yellow bill. Mostly heard calling from dense reedbeds but will enter open areas where it may be seen dashing about with rapid movements. 20 cm

Helmeted Guineafowl

A well-known game bird naturally occurring in bushveld and on arable land, where groups of up to 20 birds typically run together. From a distance appears mostly grey but at close range the finely white-dotted plumage is visible. Naked blue and red head distinctive. 56 cm

Ground Hornbill

An easily recognized, turkey-sized bird with a long bill and conspicuous red face and throat patch; commonly occurs in small family groups. Walks on tips of its toes. In flight shows large white wing patches. 90 cm

Southern Yellowbilled Hornbill

The long, banana-shaped, yellow bill is diagnostic. Plumage is speckled black and white, and tail is long and narrow. Common in bushveld and large game reserves where it is a frequent visitor to restcamps. 55 cm

African Jacana

A distinctive wetland bird with a rufous body, a buffy yellow collar, a white breast and throat, and a blue bill and forehead. Exceptionally long toes and nails allow it to balance on floating vegetation. 28 cm

distinctive head pattern →

Blacksmith Plover

The striking black, white and grey plumage makes this an easy bird to identify, whether standing or in flight. Its clinking alarm call is given mostly in flight. Commonly associated with wetlands. 30 cm

black cap encircled by white diagnostic →

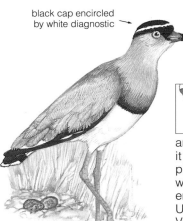

Crowned Plover

A dry-country wader, common around towns and cities where it frequents road verges and playing fields; not associated with water. White crown encircling head is diagnostic. Utters a harsh alarm call. Very active at night. 30 cm

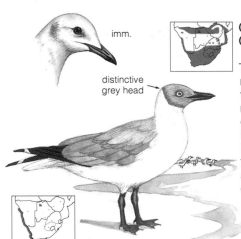

imm.

distinctive
grey head

Greyheaded Gull

The only gull commonly seen away from the coast. Unmistakable with its grey head, and red bill, legs and feet. Imm. very different from ad., with only a few brown marks on the head. 42 cm

Hartlaub's Gull

The most abundant small gull on the Cape coast, very common around coastal fishing villages, harbours, picnic areas and rubbish dumps. Also may be seen flying above wheat fields near the coast, following the ploughs. Shows suggestion of a grey hood in breeding season, when legs, feet and bill assume a dull red colour. Endemic. 38 cm

Kelp Gull

A large black and white gull with an orange-tipped yellow bill, common on all coasts. Breeds on offshore islands and typically gathers in large numbers to scavenge in fishing harbours and rubbish dumps. Imm. is dark brown, lightening with age. 60 cm

Cape Turtle Dove

A common bird in most towns and cities and very abundant in the bush-veld. Smaller and paler than Redeyed Dove, and shows much more white on the tail. Differs from Laughing Dove by having thin, black half-collar on hind neck. 28 cm

conspicuous white on tail

Redeyed Dove

Common in the south, east and north of the region where it has adapted to city gardens and parks. Much larger than similar Cape Turtle Dove; also shows grey band on tip of undertail but lacks white on uppertail. Red skin around eye visible only at close range. 35 cm

Feral Pigeon

The most common pigeon in cities and towns, descended from escaped racing pigeons. Typical bird is dark bluish-grey with black bars on wings and a white rump, but many different colour variations occur. Alien. 33 cm

pale speckling

Rock Pigeon

Well adapted to cities where it has taken to breeding on building ledges. Pale speckling on back and wings. Bare red skin around eyes, and red feet and toes are diagnostic. 33 cm

Greenspotted Dove

Very common in game reserves. In flight shows two dark bars on rump and chestnut patches on wings. 22 cm

iridescent green wing spots not easily seen

Laughing Dove

Differs from Cape Turtle Dove and Red-eyed Dove by its much smaller size and lack of black half-collar. Breast is pinkish, and cinnamon-coloured back is offset by bluish forewings. 26 cm

Burchell's Coucal

A large bird which tends to keep to thick tangles, though will often sit on a prominent perch in the early morning or after heavy rain. The chestnut back and wings and long, floppy tail help identification. 44 cm

Redchested Cuckoo

The 'piet-my-vrou' call is heard more often than the bird is seen. Typically conceals itself in tops of trees; when seen, the very dark back and rufous breast are distinctive. A common summer visitor. 30 cm

rufous breast

glossy green plumage

Diederik Cuckoo

A small, glossy green cuckoo, easily identified by its distinctive 'dee-dee-deederik' call. Often associated with reedbeds and more directly with weaver colonies, in the nests of which it lays its eggs. Summer visitor. 18 cm

erectile crest

Grey Lourie

An all-grey bird, somewhat like a giant mousebird, with a long tail and crest. Occurs in small groups in bushveld, often perched high up in thorn trees. Characteristic 'go-way' call alerts other birds to the approach of danger. 48 cm

'ear tufts'   yellow eyes

Spotted Eagle Owl

A large owl with prominent 'ear tufts', large yellow eyes and brown and black barred plumage. Well adapted to towns and cities, and may be seen out hunting in the early morning or evening. Rests in thick foliage or on cliff ledges during the day. 43-50 cm

black eyes   heart-shaped face

Barn Owl

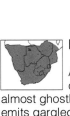

A white owl with an almost ghostly form, it emits gargled screeches and screams while hunting at night. Roosts during the day in old buildings and barns. The heart-shaped face, black eyes and pale underparts identify this owl. 34 cm

Little Swift

A small, fast-moving, black and white bird, directly associated with buildings and bridges where it breeds in colonies. During the breeding season, groups gather in flight and wheel, spiralling upwards. 14 cm

square-ended tail

Rock Martin

A swallow- or swift-like bird, generally greyish-brown and showing white spots in centre of spread tail. Found mostly in rocky or mountainous areas but has adapted to towns and cities. 15 cm

white spots on tail

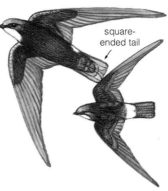

black and white beak

crest

Speckled Mousebird

A small, drab bird with a long tail and a very clumsy flight pattern. Appears to hang from branches when perched, and creeps around in foliage like a small rodent. The call is a harsh 'zhrrik-zhrrik'. 35 cm

Pied Kingfisher

A conspicuous black and white kingfisher with a long black bill; occurs mostly in small groups. Male has double black breast band, and female has single band. Typically hovers above water before plunging in to catch fish. 28 cm

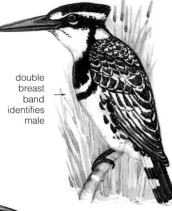

double breast band identifies male

flash of blue on wings and rump

Brownhooded Kingfisher

A drab, brown and grey kingfisher with a long red bill. Found away from water in open woodland and coastal forests. Also has adapted to suburban parks and gardens. Catches insects and reptiles from an exposed perch. 24 cm

shaggy crest

Malachite Kingfisher

A small, electric-blue and red bird which flies rapidly along freshwater streams and edges of reed-beds. Often darts into water from perch to catch fish, sometimes hovering briefly before plunging in. 14 cm

Lilacbreasted Roller

large head and bill

Often perches prominently on telephone poles and wires from where it hunts insects. In flight, especially in 'rolling' display, the combination of blues, lilac and chestnut make this bird unmistakable. Distinguished from similar European Roller by its long outertail feathers. 36 cm

holds crest erect when alarmed

conspicuous zig-zag pattern on wings

Hoopoe

Typically flies with jerky, butterfly-like movements and raises crest on landing. Feeds on the ground, probing bill into the earth for food. Gives a soft 'hoop-hoop-hoop' call. 28 cm

decurved red bill

Redbilled Woodhoopoe

The oily, bottle-green and blue plumage, long red bill and long white-tipped tail are diagnostic. Occurs in small groups or family parties, which often utter a vigorous cackling chatter in unison. 36 cm

Blackcollared Barbet

A bulbul-sized barbet with a stumpy tail, a very thick, short bill, and a bright red face and throat bordered by a broad black collar. Imm. is dowdier and has a brown face streaked with red. Occurs in small parties, or in pairs which call to each other in a duet. 20 cm

bright head pattern ←

distinctive shaggy crest →

Crested Barbet

Larger than Blackcollared Barbet, with bright orange, yellow, red and black plumage and a shaggy crest; shows general black and white chequered pattern in flight. Has a rapid, continuous trilling call. Primarily a bushveld bird but does frequent gardens. 23 cm

Whitefronted Bee-eater

Found mostly in small groups near rivers and in damp areas. The bright crimson and white throat combined with blue undertail and green back are diagnostic. Imm. is a duller version of ad. Nests in sandbanks. 24 cm

crimson and white throat →

Cardinal Woodpecker

The smallest wood-pecker in the region, easily recognized by its barred brown and white back. Progresses up tree trunks with short, jerky movements, stopping at intervals to tap rapidly with its bill. 15 cm

male has red nape

European Swallow

The diagnostic brick-red head and throat, and black breast band are visible at close range. Remaining underparts are creamy-white and the upper-parts are a glossy, dark blue. Tail is long and forked. May occur in vast numbers, and often seen resting in long rows on tele-phone wires. Summer visitor. 18 cm

Greater Striped Swallow

A large swallow with finely streaked underparts and an orange rump and cap. Often found along roadways where it breeds in drain-pipes and stormwater drains. Summer visitor. 20 cm

finely streaked underparts

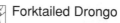

Forktailed Drongo

Common and conspicuous in most areas, often seen perched on telephone wires. Easily recognized by the all-black plumage and deeply forked tail. Its call is sharp and harsh. Often chases birds larger than itself, such as crows and raptors. 25 cm

Pied Crow

Except at long range when it might be mistaken for another crow species, this bird is unmistakable with its distinctive black and white plumage. Mostly keeps to open veld and woodlands, although is now found in towns and cities. Its call is a deep, guttural 'caw-caw'.
50 cm

dagger-shaped bill

Black Crow

A large, all-black bird usually found in pairs in open veld areas, cultivated fields and dry desert regions. The long, dagger-shaped bill and shaggy throat feathers are diagnostic. Imm. is generally duller than ad. Its call is a garbled jumble of notes.
50 cm

Blackheaded Oriole

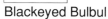

The male is a bright, all-yellow bird with black wings and head, and a coral-red bill; female is a dull yellowish-olive. The call is a fluty and melodic short phrase. Birds usually solitary or found in pairs. 24 cm

Blackeyed Bulbul

Very similar to the Cape and Redeyed bulbuls (both endemics), each species having a dark head and a yellow vent. Species differ mainly in the colour of the eye wattle: the Blackeyed Bulbul has a black, the Redeyed Bulbul has a red, and the Cape Bulbul has a bright white eye wattle. 21 cm

Redeyed Bulbul

Cape Bulbul

Cape Rock Thrush

Chat-like in shape, and found on rocky hillsides at the coast and inland. Male has a blue-grey head, throat and upper breast, and orange underparts. Female has a mottled black and white head, but also shows orange underparts and tail. Endemic. 21 cm

pale blue head

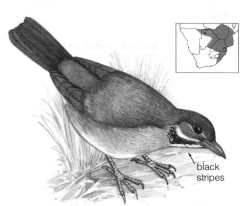

Kurrichane Thrush

Resembles Olive Thrush but has a bright orange bill and noticeable black moustachial stripes. Found in open woodland but has also adapted to towns and cities. 22 cm

black stripes

speckled throat

Olive Thrush

A secretive forest bird which has adapted to gardens and parks. Easily recognized by the yellow bill, speckled throat and overall darkish colour. Typically hops along the ground, turning leaves in search of food.
24 cm

rufous throat

Cape Robin

Although normally shy in its river-ine and forest habitat, now common in some suburban gardens. When startled, will fly for cover showing its red tail with a dark centre. 18 cm

Cape Wagtail

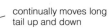
continually moves long tail up and down

A small bird with a long tail, which it continually moves up and down whether foraging or at rest. Mostly grey above and white below with a black breast band and a narrow white eyebrow stripe. Once common in parks and gardens, its numbers were depleted by man's use of insecticides. Occurs naturally in marshy areas. 18 cm

Grassveld Pipit

The most common pipit in the region, occurring in grassy areas. Plain greyish-brown with streaks; shows conspicuous white outer tail feathers. In display flight ascends and then spirals slowly downwards. 16 cm

orange throat diagnostic →

Orangethroated Longclaw

Could be confused with a pipit when viewed from behind, but underparts are yellowish and the throat is an almost luminescent orange encircled with black. In flight shows white tip to the tail. Has a cat-like nasal call. Endemic. 20 cm

Bokmakierie

A brightly coloured, yellow and green shrike with a broad black breast band. In flight shows a yellow tip to its long green tail. A very vocal bird, with pairs performing complex duets. Found in mountain and coastal scrub. Endemic. 23 cm

♂

Fiscal Shrike

One of the region's best known birds, it commonly sits exposed on poles, fences and telephone wires. The black and white plumage and long tail help to identify this shrike; in addition the female shows a rufous flank patch. The bill is powerful and hooked for tearing apart its prey. 23 cm

♀

imm. has brown plumage and grey underparts

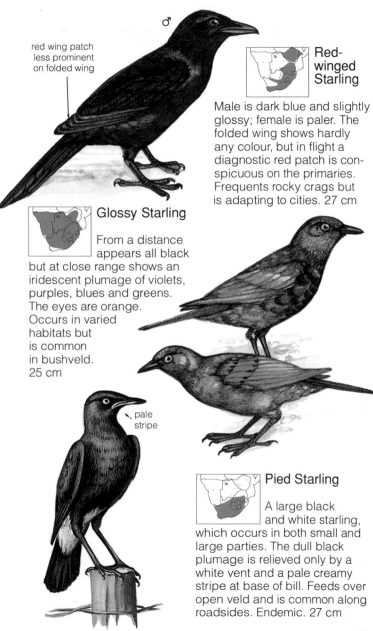

red wing patch less prominent on folded wing

♂

Red-winged Starling

Male is dark blue and slightly glossy; female is paler. The folded wing shows hardly any colour, but in flight a diagnostic red patch is conspicuous on the primaries. Frequents rocky crags but is adapting to cities. 27 cm

Glossy Starling

From a distance appears all black but at close range shows an iridescent plumage of violets, purples, blues and greens. The eyes are orange. Occurs in varied habitats but is common in bushveld. 25 cm

pale stripe

Pied Starling

A large black and white starling, which occurs in both small and large parties. The dull black plumage is relieved only by a white vent and a pale creamy stripe at base of bill. Feeds over open veld and is common along roadsides. Endemic. 27 cm

39

Plumcoloured Starling

Male is very distinctive with glossy violet upperparts and head; the female is mottled and streaked dark brown above, and the white underparts are heavily streaked with brown. Occurs in various wooded habitats as a summer visitor. 19 cm

European Starling

A small, dark starling which from a distance appears all black. At close range plumage looks oily and iridescent, showing shades of dark blue, green and black, with buff tips to feathers imparting a speckled look. A noisy, gregarious bird, sometimes occurring in large flocks. Alien. 21 cm

Indian Myna

A brownish bird with a glossy black head, a bright yellow bill, and bare skin around the eyes, and on the legs and feet. In flight shows conspicuous white wing patches and white tail tip. Common to abundant in some areas, and usually occurs in roosts of up to several thousand. Feeds in open grassy areas. Alien. 25 cm

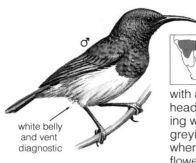

Whitebellied Sunbird

A small sunbird with a bottle-green and blue head and back, and a contrasting white belly; female is drab greyish-brown. Very active when feeding, flitting from flower to flower. 11 cm

white belly and vent diagnostic

Cape Sugarbird

Commonly seen in stands of proteas in the southern Cape. Male is conspicuous, with an extremely long tail; female has a shorter tail but, like the male, shows a yellow vent and a decurved bill. Endemic. 29 cm

gleaming colours

long tail →

Black Sunbird

A drab, matt-black sunbird with a bright, shiny purple throat and an iridescent blue and green forehead; female is drab brown with streaked underparts. 15 cm

41

House Sparrow

Very widespread and rarely found away from human habitation. Male has a grey cap, black bib and chestnut shoulder; female is drab mousy-brown and grey. Both sexes show a white wing bar. Alien. 14 cm

black bib

diagnostic head pattern

Cape Sparrow

Well-established near human habitation but also found in outlying areas in open veld. Male's striking black and white head is diagnostic; female shows faint shadow markings of male's head pattern. Endemic. 15 cm

Greyheaded Sparrow

Fairly non-descript with a grey head, and a chestnut back and rump. Invariably associated with human habitation but also occurs in bushveld where it nests in hollow branches. Sexes similar, both showing creamy wing bar. 15 cm

grey head and chestnut back diagnostic

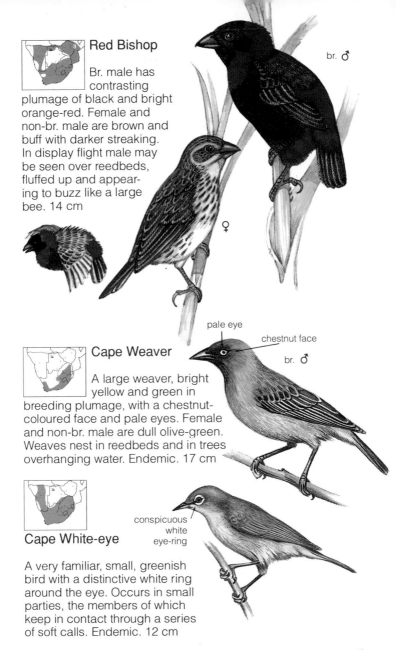

Red Bishop

Br. male has contrasting plumage of black and bright orange-red. Female and non-br. male are brown and buff with darker streaking. In display flight male may be seen over reedbeds, fluffed up and appearing to buzz like a large bee. 14 cm

br. ♂

♀

Cape Weaver

pale eye

chestnut face

br. ♂

A large weaver, bright yellow and green in breeding plumage, with a chestnut-coloured face and pale eyes. Female and non-br. male are dull olive-green. Weaves nest in reedbeds and in trees overhanging water. Endemic. 17 cm

Cape White-eye

conspicuous white eye-ring

A very familiar, small, greenish bird with a distinctive white ring around the eye. Occurs in small parties, the members of which keep in contact through a series of soft calls. Endemic. 12 cm

br. ♂

Masked Weaver

Very similar to Spottedbacked Weaver but with a uniform olive back and with more black on the head. Females of both species are dull yellow and olive-green; non-br. male and imm. resemble female. When not breeding, birds form large flocks. 15 cm

Spottedbacked Weaver

Larger and more robust in appearance than Masked Weaver, and found mostly in the east of the region. Br. male has a yellow-spotted back and less extensive black on the head than Masked Weaver. Breeds in trees, sometimes in large colonies. 17 cm

br. ♂

br. ♂

Yellowrumped Widow

Found in damp areas and on bracken-covered mountain slopes. Male is easily recognized, with its bright yellow rump and shoulders in both breeding and non-breeding plumages; female is streaked, drab brown with traces of a yellow rump. 15 cm

Redcollared Widow

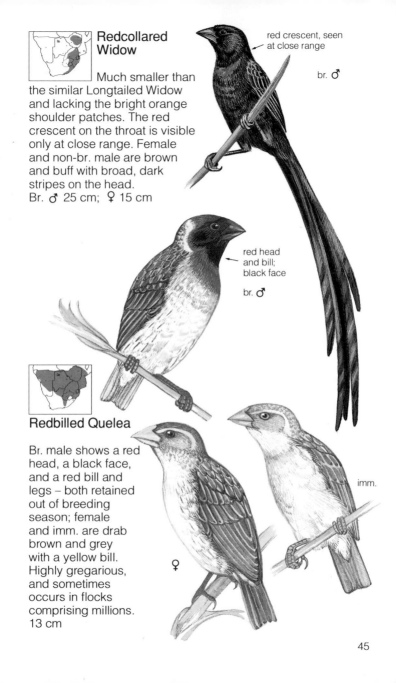

Much smaller than the similar Longtailed Widow and lacking the bright orange shoulder patches. The red crescent on the throat is visible only at close range. Female and non-br. male are brown and buff with broad, dark stripes on the head.
Br. ♂ 25 cm; ♀ 15 cm

red crescent, seen at close range

br. ♂

red head and bill; black face

br. ♂

Redbilled Quelea

Br. male shows a red head, a black face, and a red bill and legs – both retained out of breeding season; female and imm. are drab brown and grey with a yellow bill. Highly gregarious, and sometimes occurs in flocks comprising millions.
13 cm

♀

imm.

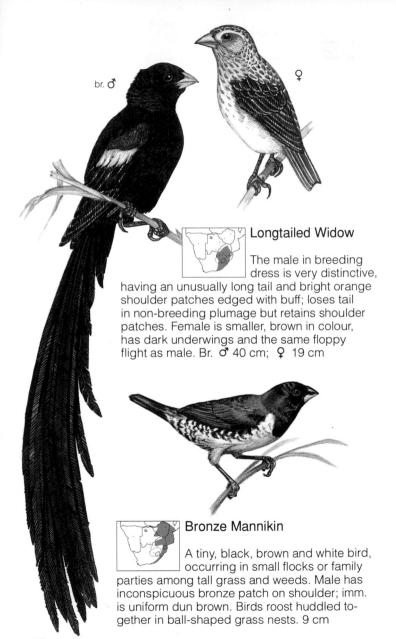

br. ♂

♀

Longtailed Widow

The male in breeding dress is very distinctive, having an unusually long tail and bright orange shoulder patches edged with buff; loses tail in non-breeding plumage but retains shoulder patches. Female is smaller, brown in colour, has dark underwings and the same floppy flight as male. Br. ♂ 40 cm; ♀ 19 cm

Bronze Mannikin

A tiny, black, brown and white bird, occurring in small flocks or family parties among tall grass and weeds. Male has inconspicuous bronze patch on shoulder; imm. is uniform dun brown. Birds roost huddled together in ball-shaped grass nests. 9 cm

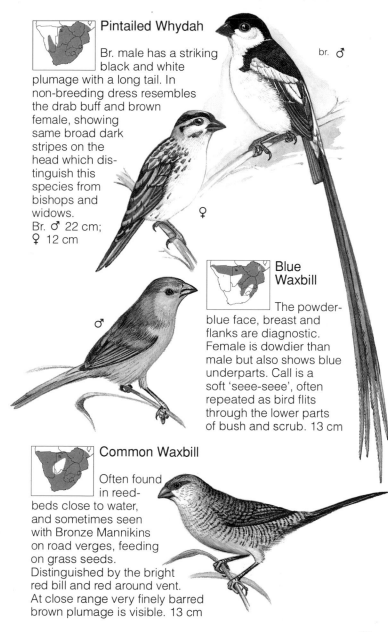

Pintailed Whydah

br. ♂

Br. male has a striking black and white plumage with a long tail. In non-breeding dress resembles the drab buff and brown female, showing same broad dark stripes on the head which distinguish this species from bishops and widows.
Br. ♂ 22 cm;
♀ 12 cm

♀

Blue Waxbill

♂

The powder-blue face, breast and flanks are diagnostic. Female is dowdier than male but also shows blue underparts. Call is a soft 'seee-seee', often repeated as bird flits through the lower parts of bush and scrub. 13 cm

Common Waxbill

Often found in reed-beds close to water, and sometimes seen with Bronze Mannikins on road verges, feeding on grass seeds. Distinguished by the bright red bill and red around vent. At close range very finely barred brown plumage is visible. 13 cm

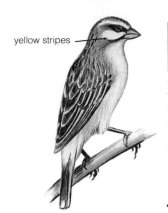

yellow stripes

Yelloweyed Canary

When flushed from grassy road verges by passing traffic, bright yellow rump and yellow-tipped tail are seen. Sexes are similar, both having bright yellow underparts and yellow stripes above and below the eye. 12 cm

grey nape

♂

Cape Canary

Widespread in mountainous areas but also occurs in coastal regions of the Cape. Male easily recognized by combination of grey on nape and yellow on forehead. Female and imm. are drabber and show streaking on breast. 13 cm

black and white patterned head

♂

Goldenbreasted Bunting

Male has a bright golden, almost orange breast, a chestnut mantle and a black and white patterned head; female and imm. are duller. Most often seen foraging on the ground in woodland, and when disturbed will fly for cover into nearby canopy. 16 cm

Birdwatching by habitat

Most birds have a preferred habitat, that is, an area associated with a particular type of vegetation or, in the case of an estuary, lake or ocean, a distinct environment within a vegetation zone. Some birds may occupy a range of habitats, but this is unusual and most show a preference for one area over another. Various species have adapted to man-altered habitats, such as cities and gardens, but in many cases these areas resemble the favoured habitat of that species.

General habitats, such as wetlands, forests and mountains, are easy to define and recognize, but some species keep to more limited and less distinct habitats, which may in fact form part of a larger habitat; these areas are more difficult to define and take time and patience to become familiar with.

Why watch birds by habitat? This approach to birding and identification can go a long way in helping the beginner sift through the confusing array of nearly 900 bird species found in southern Africa. Once you can identify different habitats, you can learn what kind of birds are generally associated with them. If you plan an outing to a very definite locality, find out what sort of habitat it represents – perhaps it is forest, marsh or scrub – and familiarize yourself with the range of birds you are likely to encounter there. With the species earmarked in your guide, you will save considerable time in looking for a bird you want to identify.

The habitats of southern Africa and some of the birds found in each are as follows:

Wetlands

These include marshes, reedbeds, ponds, dams and any open stretch of fresh water, even down to your local reservoir or sewage works. The birds most likely to be seen here are waterbirds, but in most cases the immediate surrounds will support a selection of grassland species too. If the water levels are low, you will find some wading birds, including the Grey Heron, Great White Egret, and possibly an African Spoonbill, a Sacred Ibis or a Hamerkop. Smaller wading birds, found on gravel and in muddy areas, would include the Blacksmith and Trebleblanded plovers and the Wood Sandpiper, and the only gull likely to be seen would be the Greyheaded Gull.

Typical wetland setting

On the open stretches of water look out for different duck species: in the deeper parts the Southern Pochard and Maccoa Duck, and in shallower water around the edges, the dabbling ducks: Redbilled, Cape and Hottentot teals and the Yellowbilled Duck. The Dabchick and other grebes might occur and also the various cormorants and the Darter. Depending on the size of the wetland, you might find White or Pinkbacked Pelican and Greater Flamingo. Also, emerging from the reedbanks may be Redknobbed Coot, Moorhen, Purple Gallinule or Black Crake, and on sandbars or floating vegetation an African Jacana, Egyptian Goose or Spurwinged Goose. Smaller birds associated with the reeds may include the European Swallow, which roosts there in the evenings, the Red Bishop and the Common Waxbill. During the dry season, the diversity of bird species in wetland areas is greatly increased, as virtually any species may arrive to drink; this may happen regardless of season in desert or semi-desert areas.

Yellowbilled Ducks (keep to shallow water)

Birdwatching can be done successfully at any time of the day in wetlands although, for maximum activity and song, the early morning is most advantageous. Always try to position yourself with the sun behind you, so as to ensure the best light conditions; and remember to take binoculars or a telescope for viewing birds in the distance. This kind of habitat can be most rewarding, and for those who do not have access to the coast it is a very good substitute.

Coasts and estuaries
Birdwatching in this habitat is greatly influenced by two important factors, namely, the province in which the coastal area occurs, and the time of year at which you set out to watch birds. The Cape coast supports quite different bird species from the more tropical Natal coast, the southern and western Cape coasts being very much richer in local breeding species than those of Natal. Season also affects the diversity and number of birds occurring in this habitat, and in summer there are much better viewing opportunities because of the additional migrant species which arrive from the northern hemisphere.

Estuaries and coastal saltpans often support a great number of birds but with little diversity in species. Large numbers of Greater and Lesser flamingos and White Pelicans may occur, as well as a selection of migrant wading birds, such as Curlew Sandpiper, Grey Plover and Little Stints. Coastal sandbars are often collecting points for the different gulls and terns.

Tide also plays an important role in a coastal habitat, and the best time to visit an estuary is on an incoming tide, when wading birds gradually move closer to shore ahead of the advancing water. They are best observed at high tide when they gather in tightly packed flocks to rest, and before they move off to feed when the tide turns. Among the better areas for birdwatching in these environments are the rocky headlands and tidal pools, where various species of roosting cormorants and birds such as the Black Oystercatcher gather. The open sandy seashore is not generally good for birds, although sanderlings and sandplovers will be seen here. On windy days it is worthwhile looking seawards, as occasionally gannets and Blackbrowed Albatross can be seen flying close inshore.

Woodlands

This is a very broad term and covers a wide variety of forest- and bush-type vegetation and habitats. Different types of woodland are associated with different bird species, so before visiting an area in this category, try and establish what sort of woodland it is, as this will give you some idea of what birds to look for. Planted forests of pine and bluegum are easy to identify as the trees are normally in rows and there is very little undergrowth. Unless such plantations have been neglected and a thick understorey has become established, your chances of seeing many bird species will be very poor. Doves, canaries and several hawk species are among the few birds you will encounter. Natural woodland, on the other hand – recognized by the diversity of tree species and their varied shapes and sizes – is likely to offer a rich birding experience. It can be very frustrating though, when an abundance of bird calls can be heard but very little is seen through the dense foliage. Initially, it is best to find a secluded spot and to sit very quietly and wait for the birds to pass. By moving through the undergrowth, you will only scare off the birds and will hear and see very little. A good time to visit a woodland is in the non-breeding season, which in most areas is in winter though it does vary from region to region. At this time birds of different species gather and form feeding flocks or 'bird parties', which move noisily through the woodland, some feeding high up in the canopy but many feeding closer to the ground and thus easily visible. If you encounter one of these parties, it is advisable to stay with it for as long as possible, and to gradually identify the many species that make up the group.

One of the best types of woodland in which to see birds is bushveld – a mixture of *Acacia* and broadleafed woodland – which is far more open than coastal, riverine or montane forest. Bushveld supports a variety of birds including rollers, barbets, woodpeckers and eagles. In the denser forest habitats, where birds are often obscured, a tape recording of bird calls is invaluable for luring the shyer species from the deep recesses of undergrowth into view.

Mountains

This includes the mountains of the southern and western Cape and the higher ranges of Natal, the Transvaal and Zimbabwe. Unlike the coastal areas, which differ widely in bird species according to province, many of the birds that occur in the mountainous areas of the Transvaal and Natal are seen in the Cape mountains and even down to sea level in the southern and western

Cape Vultures are common in mountainous regions

Cape. The Yellowrumped Widow and Cape Canary, both highland birds in Natal, are common on the Cape coast.

On the higher reaches of mountains in the region, the number of bird species found is low. Species that do occur here are most likely to be seen on crags and rocky outcrops, and include the Cape Vulture, Rock Kestrel and Rock Martin. Lower down on the heathy scrub and in gullies, the birdlife is much richer and you might find Cape Robin, Bokmakierie, Redwinged Starling, Cape Sugarbird and Spotted Eagle Owl, the latter usually well secluded behind some rocks. When weather conditions are severe in the higher altitudes, the majority of birds move down to the lower regions and take refuge in the sheltered valleys, making these areas even richer in species and well worth visiting.

Birding in mountainous habitats can be very slow, and often great distances must be covered on foot to maximize the number of species seen. It is wise not to traverse this habitat alone, and always be prepared for any kind of weather. The best time to visit mountains in the southern regions is early winter, but those in the northern regions are more rewarding in mid-summer.

Grasslands

The true natural grasslands of southern Africa are becoming scarcer each year as land is given over to agriculture and human settlement and many of our endemic birds are disappearing with them. However, a considerable number of birds normally associated with this habitat have managed to adapt to man-altered habitats, such as pastures, fields of lucerne, and other cultivated land.

Virtually any grassland is worth visiting, although the more rough, neglected and undergrazed an area is, the more productive in bird species it will be. Grazing areas of cattle or game are likely sites for the Cattle Egret and Pied Starling, and open lucerne fields are good places to look for the White Stork and Blackheaded Heron. Freshly ploughed fields or those recently planted with crops are favoured by Blue Crane, Helmeted Guineafowl and Grassveld Pipit, and areas with tall grass cover by the Black Korhaan and Longtailed Widow. On elevated perches in grassland areas, look out for the Blackshouldered Kite and Steppe Buzzard.

Blue Cranes favour freshly ploughed fields

Birdwatching in open grasslands is much the same as around estuaries, where vast expanses often separate you from the birds. A good telescope is therefore a very useful item here and, again, it is best to observe the birds with the sun behind you. If during the dry season you notice a veld fire it is worth investigating, as a host of different birds congregate along and behind the fireline, attracted by the insects and small rodents which have been caught in the flames and which provide an instant and tasty natural braai or are flushed ('smoked out') ahead of the flames.

Gardens
Most established gardens are planted with a mixture of trees and shrubs which, even if not indigenous to the area, will attract certain birds that favour a woodland-type habitat, such as barbets, thrushes, robins and woodpeckers. The development of cities and towns, however, with their cultivated gardens, parks, playing fields and even botanical gardens, has created a unique habitat for birds, and one to which many different species have adapted. Gardens, no matter what their size, can provide endless hours of successful birdwatching, and you can play a role in determining what kind of birds visit your garden by planting trees, shrubs and flowers that attract certain types of birds. The more carefully you plan your garden 'around birds', the greater your birdwatching rewards will be.

Planting for birds

Different birds are attracted to different types of trees and shrubs, depending on their diet and other habits: for example, fruit- and berry-bearing trees provide food for bulbuls, while flower-producing plants attract sunbirds and insect-eaters, which feed on the sweet nectar and the numerous insects also attracted to the nectar. Some birds are drawn to a particular tree or creeper for nesting purposes. So before planting a profusion of shrubs, trees and flowering plants, think about the type of birds you would like to attract, find out about their habits and plan your garden accordingly. The local conditions of your area (soil, rainfall, wind, etc.) will obviously influence your final choice, as plants have minimum growing requirements which must be met for them to thrive. Remember that indigenous plants will attract indigenous birds and the greater the diversity of plant species, the greater the diversity of birds you will encourage. Seek advice from your local nursery or botanic garden about plants most suited to your area.

Trees and shrubs

Fruit- and berry-eating birds – the bulbuls, barbets, louries, mousebirds and thrushes – will relish the berries produced by the various *Olea* species (Olive trees), which grow successfully in most parts of the country; the Common Tree Euphorbia (*Euphorbia ingens*) and the Wild Peach (*Kiggelaria africana*) also grow well throughout the region and offer good supplies of fruit. For areas with mild winters and plentiful annual rainfall, the Natal Plum (*Carissa macrocarpa*), *Syzygium* species (Water berry, Water pear, etc.) and milkwood trees (*Mimusops* spp.) are good choices, and the various species of indigenous fig trees (*Ficus* spp.) are supreme in encouraging wild birds, which feed not only on the fleshy fruit but also on the multitude of insects attracted to it. In areas with a harsher, drier climate, guarri trees (*Euclea* spp.) will appeal to the fruit-eaters as will the Karree (*Rhus lancea*). The slow-growing White Stinkwood (*Celtis africana*) is also an excellent fruit provider, suited to the Highveld and southern and eastern parts of the country, and a popular and easily grown, berry-laden tree is the Pigeonwood (*Trema orientalis*).

Mousebirds eating
papaw

Exotic fruit trees, such as the papaw, can also be planted and will please the mousebirds and barbets in your region, and Cotoneaster and Pyracantha shrubs will also draw birds to their bundles of fleshy berries.

Flowering plants

Some birds will visit the garden for the nectar-producing plants and the host of insects they attract, which also provide a meal. Sunbirds, sugarbirds, warblers and flycatchers are among these. The seed-eating weavers, white-eyes and canaries may also arrive when the flowers begin to seed. Many of the *Acacia* species are popular choices because they provide both nectar and seeds which are attractive to birds. These are hardy trees and grow well in the Highveld, Lowveld and in dry areas. Some Ericas and many Proteas are well-suited to the south-western Cape climate, and are obvious choices for attracting sugarbirds and sunbirds. Also, find out which of the Aloe species will grow in your area, as many birds are drawn to them: sunbirds utilize the plant for its nectar and warblers feed on the insects attracted to its flowers. In warm tropical and subtropical climates, Gardenias will thrive and draw birds to their flowers, nectar and fruit, and the attractive Wild Dagga plant (*Leonotis leonurus*) will supply plentiful nectar. The Sausage Tree (*Kigelia africana*) also produces ample nectar and grows well in the Lowveld, and creepers like the Cape Honeysuckle (*Tecomaria capensis*), which is successfully grown along the coast, are invaluable for covering unsightly fences as well as for the nectar they produce.

The real bird enthusiast will leave a section of the garden to run wild, to encourage thicket growth and so provide cover for the more furtive bird species. Grasses left to grow tall and bear feathery seeded heads in this area will prove irresistible to canaries, bishops, weavers and Bronze Mannikins, and the areas of dense bush will be favoured by the shyer robins and the Bokmakierie.

Other ways of attracting birds to the garden

While propagating indigenous plant species to attract birds is very successful, there are several other ways of encouraging more birds to the garden: you can feed them, provide water for drinking and bathing, and create conditions suitable for nesting.

Feeding

If you are intending to feed birds regularly, it is no use scattering breadcrumbs or other kitchen discards on a bare piece of lawn near the house: this will leave the birds open to attack from predators such as cats, and the food will encourage the unwelcome interest of rodents. The basic requirement for feeding birds is a simple bird table, raised high enough above the ground to allow the birds to feed without threat from domestic animals. A straight, stout pole with a square of wood nailed on top will suffice, and is even better if bordered by a narrow skirting to prevent the food from falling or blowing off. Bird tables can be far more elaborate of course, and may have various levels for feeding, a roof

Basic feeding platform secured to a pole

for protection from the elements, or a slate slab in place of a wooden one. The essential factor is that the feeding surface is raised, and preferably located in partial shade. Bear in mind that you will want to watch the birds feeding, so place the table within good viewing distance of a window, and if you intend photographing different species, take into consideration the lighting conditions at different times of the day and in different seasons.

Other devices can be constructed or bought for feeding birds, many of which overcome the problem of bullying by larger birds over smaller ones, often seen at bird tables. Among the most successful of these are the 'hanging feeders': the platform-type is easily made from a square of wood or slate, attached at each corner to a piece of wire and suspended from a branch. Another type of hanging feeder can be made by filling a mesh bag (such as those in which onions and potatoes are bought) with suitable food, tightly closing it and hanging it from a branch. This type of feeder effectively excludes the

'Mesh-bag' hanging feeder

more aggressive birds, such as doves, Mynas and starlings, and gives the smaller white-eyes, bulbuls and weavers a chance to feed without intrusions.

Seed-eating birds are also often discouraged from feeding at bird tables by larger, more dominant birds. The more vulnerable species can be encouraged by hanging commercial seed dispensers such as those used in bird cages, which are specially designed for smaller birds. These work on the gravity principle, a tube-like container holding a large amount of seed which is dispensed from below through a small projecting lip. These feeders are very economical when compared with a table where seed is so easily blown away or dispersed by the busy activity of the birds.

With patience you can also attract sunbirds through artificial feeding. Use the same gravity feeders described above (the more brightly coloured the better), fill them with a thick solution of sugar water or glucose water, and hang them from the trees. If this does not attract the birds, take a few clumps of flowers from plant species that the sunbirds favour, and attach these to the dispensers; in time the birds will recognize them as a food source and will visit regularly to feed.

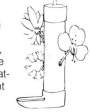

Gravity feeder

People living in flats can also draw certain birds to their window ledges and balconies by putting out trays of suitable food. Fruit-eating birds, which are usually reluctant to venture into the confined area of a balcony, can be attracted by easy-to-construct 'fruit poles': hammer nails along the length of a one-metre wooden pole, allowing them to protrude sufficiently for fruit pieces to be spiked on them, and attach the pole securely at right angles to the balcony rail. Weavers, bulbuls and barbets will not be able to resist over-ripe pieces of fruit which are offered and can safely perch on the pole while they feed.

What to feed the birds

Although kitchen scraps will not go to waste when placed on your feeders, they are not altogether suitable and do not bring the same variety of birds as more 'specialized' food does. In fact, with leftover scraps you have less control over the type of birds you attract and the result is usually one in which Mynas and starlings dominate to the exclusion of smaller species.

Small seed-eating birds will appreciate a variety of foods, including crushed barley, wheat, oats, mealies and sunflower seeds. Wild-bird seed and ordinary budgie-seed can always be bought, and will have just as much appeal. Fruit is always a temptation, particularly if it is over-ripe. Barbets, bulbuls and white-eyes will converge around offerings of apples, grapes, oranges and guavas, and a slice of soft papaw will delight the mousebirds. Insect-eating birds will flock to a supply of bone meal, which can be bought very cheaply from the butcher. A large bone, that still has pieces of fat and meat on it is also a great attraction and will be picked clean by robins, shrikes and thrushes. Lumps of suet and old fatty rinds prove very popular too.

Remember that birds fed on a regular basis in your garden will come to depend on this source of food and some may establish territories and try to raise their families there. Obviously, many birds would suffer should you discontinue the food supply for any reason. If you are going on holiday, even if just for a few days, arrange for someone to feed the birds in your absence. Alternatively, try to prevent the birds from coming to rely solely on your source of food, by offering moderate amounts each day.

Water

A garden 'planned for birds' is not complete without a supply of water, particularly in drier parts of the region. Many birds rely on water for drinking and also need to bath regularly to maintain their plumages. The simplest birdbath can be provided by inverting the lid of a plastic or metal dustbin, propping it level with bricks and filling it with water. Again, it is important to raise the bath to a height beyond the reach of potential predators. Elevated, pedestal-type birdbaths can be purchased from nurseries and large general stores, and are constructed to avoid this problem. Baths should be placed in partial shade and ideally near a tree where the birds can settle to dry out and preen after bathing. Also, to save you having to fill the bath daily, run a hose-pipe to it and leave the tap on a very slow drip.

For those with bigger properties, the ultimate in bird watering points is a pond. With a large enough area you can create a freshwater habitat, surrounded by reeds and overhanging trees. If you fill the pond with fish you may eventually attract a kingfisher, and when the frogs arrive perhaps some herons or a Hamerkop.

Pedestal-type birdbath

The garden as a breeding ground

To encourage birds to nest and breed in your garden, you need to ensure that there is plentiful food and ample potential for nesting sites – either in the form of sheltered trees and bushes or artificially constructed nesting places. Thickets and dense hedges growing in the 'wild' section of your garden should provide sufficient cover for species such as shrikes, robins and warblers, while flycatchers and wagtails will seek out nesting cover in vines and creepers, which you may have growing over a patio or along a fence.

Hole-nesting species such as barbets and woodpeckers will be drawn to dead or dying trees for nest sites. These often offer natural crevices and holes, or are decayed enough to enable the birds to excavate their own. However, a dead tree is not something you would choose for your garden, and this is where artificial nest boxes will be useful in encouraging certain species. Some of the different options are discussed below.

'Dead-branch' nests

This is one of the most natural-looking forms of artificial nesting and is probably one of the easiest to set up. It simply involves attaching a length of dead branch to a pole or living tree. It is important, however, to select a branch from the right kind of tree because if the wood is too soft it will soon begin to crumble. Among the best woods to use are willow, syringa and several species of *Acacia*. Select branches of various lengths up to two metres, and with a diameter of no less than 250 mm, and secure these firmly to a vertical trunk or branch at a height of at least two metres. The best way to fix the dead branch is with galvanized wire, which should ensure a secure attachment (no bird will take to nesting in a branch that is unstable or likely to slip). Always position the branches away from bad weather and out of direct sunlight and wind.

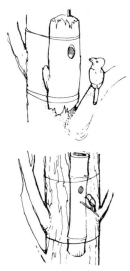

Dead-branch nests secured with galvanized wire

Barbets and woodpeckers will excavate their own entrance holes and nest chambers in the attached branches, and you may find that sparrows take over these holes once they are vacated. With a bit of luck you may even have honeyguides parasitizing one of the nests. If you wish to encourage other hole-nesting species which do not excavate their own nests (Woodhoopoe and Wryneck), use lengths of branches that are already hollow, such as those of bamboo or sisal plants, and drill a hole about 25-30 mm in diameter a third of the way down the branch. Again, attach the nests with galvanized wire and position them away from the bright sunlight and wind.

'Hollow tree' nests

Other bird species, such as wood-hoopoes, are also hole-nesting but usually locate hollow boles in trees which are much larger in diameter than a 'dead branch' nest could viably be. These nesting cavities can be mimicked by constructing a box out of pine, about one metre long, 200 mm wide and 200 mm high. The roof of the box should slant slightly forward to allow any rainwater to run of, and an  entrance hole about 50 mm in diameter must be cut in the front a third of the way from the top. You can also attach a small perch below the entrance hole to give the bird a post for landing before entering the nest. The whole structure should be painted or stained in a colour that will blend with surrounding vegetation and bark.

Much smaller versions of these boxes can be constructed for smaller birds, but remember to keep the entrance hole proportionally small so as to prevent unwanted large birds from entering the nest.

Owl boxes

If you live on a large plot or in a less built-up area, you may have seen owls in the vicinity, and can try and encourage these birds to roost or nest in your garden by constructing artificial nesting boxes. The size of your property will dictate how many nest boxes to construct and how far apart to place them: one owl requires an area of approximately one hectare. The boxes will have to be fairly substantial in size and will require a large entrance hole in front. For a Barn Owl, which nests naturally in a tree cavity or hole, a box with dimensions 500 mm x 300 mm x 250 mm is ideal, and should be attached to a large tree at a height of at least six metres. A Spotted Eagle Owl is of course a much larger bird and although it would make use of a nest box, it would require such a large one that

Owl box set high up in tree

it would be impractical both in terms of construction and placing. You can accommodate this bird by placing a large wooden platform (600 x 300 mm, with a skirting of 200 mm) high up in a tall tree.

To further enhance their suitability as roosting or nesting sites, line the bases of the boxes or platforms with small wooden chippings and a few twigs.

With a little extra effort you can fit a two-way mirror into a nest box. This will allow you to look into the nest cavity and follow the breeding cycle without undue disturbance of the birds; at night you can use a torch to watch the proceedings. Take care to always approach the nest very quietly and not to alarm the birds in any way; they are very quick to desert, especially during the early stages of breeding.

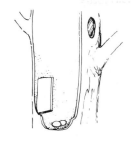

Nest hole fitted with two-way mirror

Having succeeded in attracting a variety of birds to your garden, you can now sit back and enjoy them, photographing them in different seasons and learning more about their habits. You can be more scientific of course, and keep notes on their behaviour, breeding biology and display. Once you can identify all the species visiting your garden, you may want to keep a weekly or monthly log, noting the times at which different birds visit and the numbers that arrive. After doing this for a few years you will be able to see definite patterns emerging for each species, which may reveal something about different birds' local and long-distance movements (through arrival and departure dates), general seasonal abundance, or even something about countrywide weather cycles (droughts and wet periods). The rewards of attracting and watching birds in your garden are many, and you will be surprised to see how many species have adapted to and will visit the city or suburban garden.

Glossary

Alien A bird which is not indigenous to the area.
Call Short notes given by males and females for alarm and contact purposes (*see* Song).
Cap Area encompassing forehead and crown.
Cere Coloured bare skin at the base of the upper mandible in raptors.
Crest Elongated feathers on the forehead, crown or nape.
Endemic Restricted to a certain region.
Eye-ring Circle of coloured feathers immediately around the eye.
Flight pattern The diagnostic pattern of a bird in flight.
Immature A bird that has moulted its juvenile plumage but has not yet attained full adult plumage.
Juvenile The first full-feathered plumage of a young bird.
Migrant A species that undertakes long-distance flights between its wintering and breeding areas.
Moustachial stripes Lines running from the base of the bill to the sides of the throat (*see* malar region in illustration).
Parasitize When a bird lays its eggs in the nest of another species for the purposes of incubation.
Plumage Feathering of a kind.
Primaries The outermost major flight feathers of the wing.
Resident A bird that occurs throughout the year in a region and is not known to undertake migration.
Roost To sleep or rest either in flocks or singly.
Secondaries Flight feathers of the wing adjoining the primaries.
Song A series of notes given by the male to proclaim his territory (*see* Call).
Summer visitor A bird that is absent from the region during the winter months, having migrated to breed in the northern hemisphere or to spend the winter months in central Africa.
Territory An area that a bird establishes and subsequently defends from others.
Vent Area from the belly to the undertail coverts.

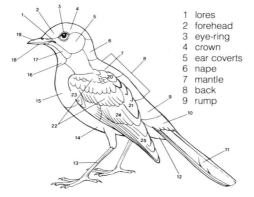

1 lores	10 uppertail coverts
2 forehead	11 tail
3 eye-ring	12 undertail coverts
4 crown	13 tarsus
5 ear coverts	14 belly
6 nape	15 breast
7 mantle	16 throat
8 back	17 malar region
9 rump	18 lower mandible
	19 upper mandible
	20 scapulars
	21 tertials
	22 wing coverts
	23 alula
	24 secondaries
	25 primaries

Further reading

Dobinson, H.H. 1976. *Bird Count* Penguin Books, England.
Maclean, G.L. (5th ed., 1984) *Roberts' Birds of Southern Africa*
The Trustees of the John Voelcker Bird Book Fund, Cape Town.
Newman, K.B. 1983. *Newman's Birds of Southern Africa* Macmillan
South Africa, Johannesburg.
Sinclair, I. (2nd ed., 1987). *Field Guide to the Birds of Southern Africa*
Struik, Cape Town.
Sinclair, I. and Goode, D. 1986. *Birds of Prey* Struik Pocket Guides for
Southern Africa, Struik, Cape Town.
Soper, T. 1978. *Bird Gardener's Handbook* David & Charles, England.
Spence, T. 1985. *Gardening with Birds* Delta Books, Johannesburg.

Societies, clubs and their publications

Southern African Ornithological Society, P.O. Box 87234, Houghton
2041. (Publishes *Ostrich* and *Birding in South Africa.*)
Northern Transvaal Ornithological Society, P.O. Box 4158, Pretoria
0001. (Publishes *Laniarius.*)
Witwatersrand Bird Club, P.O. Box 72091, Parkview 2122. (Publishes
WBC News-sheet.)
Cape Bird Club, P.O. Box 5022, Cape Town 8000. (Publishes
Promerops.)
Eastern Cape Bird Club, P.O. Box 27454, Greenacres 6057. (Publishes
Bee-eater.)
Natal Bird Club, P.O. Box 4085, Durban 4000. (Publishes *Albatross*
and *Fret.*)
Orange Free State Ornithological Society, P.O. Box 6614, Bloemfontein
9300.
Zimbabwe Ornithological Society, P.O. Box 8382, Causeway,
Zimbabwe. (Publishes *Honeyguide.*)
SWA/Namibia Bird Club, P.O. Box 67, Windhoek 9000. (Publishes
Lanioturdus.)
The Wildlife Society of Southern Africa, which has branches throughout
South Africa, also promotes birding.

Index/checklist of bird species

Numbers printed in **bold** refer to main species entries.
The boxes can be used to check off any birds that have been seen.